THE SAMURAI
Japan's Warriors

Robyn Watts

KNOWLEDGE
BOOKS

Teacher Notes:

Students will have the opportunity to learn about Japan's ancient history and the incredible Samurai culture that was such an important part of it. Their skills with traditional and very deadly Japanese weapons are explored, along with the responsibilities they held for their masters and the people they protected. The values of loyalty, devotion, trust and commitment can also be explored.

Discussion points for consideration:

1. Why were the Samurai such an important part of Japanese history and culture?

2. Compare and contrast the roles of the Samurai and the medieval knights. How were they alike and different?

3. Japanese history and culture continues to be a big drawcard for tourism today. Discuss this further.

Difficult words to be introduced and practiced before reading this book:

Japanese, backpacker, university, powerful, Singapore, armor, accuracy, naginata, distance, beautiful, everywhere, important, gatherers, different, peasants, merchants, protected, struggle, treatment, special, hundreds, victory, maintaining, problems, guard, soldiers, foreigners, bushido, ancient, samurai, ronin, shoguns, emperor, loyalty, swordsmith, longbow, incredible, dangerous.

Contents

1. Ancient Japan

Japan is a beautiful country. The people are friendly and kind. The cities are jammed with new tech. We see their comics everywhere. How did Japan start? What made it a great country? Why were the samurai important?

People have been living in Japan for a very long time. People have been living there for over 30,000 years, and maybe even longer.

These early people, the Jomon people, came across from Siberia during the Ice Ages. There were land bridges as the seas were lower than they are today. The Jomon people were hunters and gatherers.

The Ainu nation people of Japan seem to have come from the Jomon.

The Ainu people were like the Jomon in that they were hunters and fishers.

The Ainu were in the north islands and the new people were in the south. There were people coming across the land bridge to Japan.

These people may be what Japan is today. A mix of the first peoples and the new peoples.

2. Japanese Life

In Japan, groups of people were organised differently to how they were in Europe. The most important people were the shoguns and the lords. These were the rulers of Japan.

The peasants in Europe were the lowest group. In Japan they were not the lowest. People who produced food were very important in Japan.

Merchants - people who sold food - were the lowest group. The rice growers and food makers were higher than the sellers.

Above these people were the samurai. They were very important. They kept the peace and protected the people.

The merchants were not well-liked. They were taking other people's work and making a profit. Merchants were the lowest group.

Artists were well-liked but were not as important as farmers. Artists made swords, boats, cooking bowls and pots, clothes and art pieces.

Above the samurai at the top were the shogun or the landlords. If a samurai was walking along a street, people had to bow to him. If you did not bow he was permitted to cut your head off.

Today, farmers are still given special treatment in Japan. Farmers are important because they feed the Japanese people.

9

There were two major parts of Japan's history. The times of war and the times of peace.

During times of war, there was a struggle for power between groups. These battles went on for hundreds of years. The samurai became very important and had to do a lot of fighting.

Once the shogun was victorious and had control of Edo, the capital of Japan, there was peace for 250 years.

During times of peace, the samurai were still important. They helped maintain order. The samurai became like a member of council. He could try and fix problems for the people.

11

3. The Samurai

Samurai is the Japanese word for a warrior or guard. The samurai was paid by the warlord or landlord of that area.

The lord or landowner used the samurai to help keep control. Guarding and fighting were done by the samurai.

Japan was at war with groups trying to take control. This lasted a long time. Japan formed into a nation by the year 1600, and it had an emperor at the top. The power was with the shogun and the landlords.

The shogun and the landlords ran the country. The samurai were the police and soldiers of Japan for a long time.

Japan started to advance rapidly. It was peaceful for 250 years.

The Japanese culture we see today began and grew in this period. Nearly 40,000 samurai kept Japan peaceful.

Japan was cut off from the rest of the world. The shogun and landlords did not want foreigners coming to Japan. The traders were not allowed to leave Japan and the ports stopped any foreign ships.

The local landlords paid the shogun taxes by growing food. This money was used to keep the power with these groups.

The landlords became rich from the land and had castles and houses that showed their power.

4. Samurai Code of Bushido

The way the samurai behaved was called the Bushido. If you broke these rules you were no longer a samurai. The rules were as follows:

· Live as a samurai.

· Show loyalty to their lord. This was very important and could not be changed.

· Show no concern about pain.

· Be a samurai for life.

· Be fearless in battle and never be a coward.

· Always live with other samurai.

The samurai were a special group of people. If your father was a samurai, then you could become a samurai.

The samurai were important. They kept the peace and fought off attacks. They were allowed to have two swords.

The samurai had other jobs to do besides fighting. They also had to manage the local people in the area to get things done.

The importance of the samurai has never left Japan. Today, many see working for a Japanese business as being a samurai. Being loyal and giving your very best.

5. Samurai Armor and Weapons

There were many different weapons. Samurai armor changed over time. The samurai travelled by walking or on horseback.

Their helmet was called a Kabuto. It was made from iron or leather pieces. These pieces were tied together with steel.

At the bottom of the helmet were leather pieces like a curtain. The leather was stiff to stop sword blows.

A face plate was added. These could be very scary. On the top of the helmet you had ID markers like disks and horns, so you did not hit your own team.

The body armor fully covered the legs, arms, head and body. This helped to stop sword blows and knife attacks.

The chest armor was made of leather pieces or iron plates. The iron stopped musket shots. ID marks were added to make sure you knew who was on your side.

The lower body had iron or leather plates that hung from the chest armor. These protected the upper legs and thighs from sword hits.

Gloves with sleeves were worn to stop getting cut on the hands. These gloves were made with cloth and plates of steel.

Samurai armor also copied ideas from Europe. The steel chest plate was changed from a knights' armor to the samurai form.

Muskets were brought to Japan from Europe. The armor had to change to stop bullets.

ID was very important. The flag you see above the samurai is for telling other samurai who is on their side. The samurai also used colors and cloth to make sure the right person was attacked. This included colored armor, crests, tassels and flags.

The weapons that the samurai used were many and changing, but there were some common ones.

The samurai sword changed to the final shape which was a curved sword. This had a single sharp edge. The grip was very long which allowed space for two hands to grip. This sword was called the *katana.*

This was a faster weapon because the sword could be drawn faster. It was made with care. To stop it breaking easily, it had to be made in a special way. The person making these was called a swordsmith.

The samurai was also allowed to carry a smaller knife, like a dagger.

Other weapons used by the samurai included support weapons, muskets and longbows.

The longbow was an incredible weapon. The samurai could fire an arrow while riding a horse. It was a dangerous weapon which could cut through some of the armor.

The longbow was made from leather, cane and wood. It could be carried or fired from a sled. The musket replaced the longbow as a weapon, but it was still very important. Longbows were very accurate up to 300 ft. The skill of the archer was also very important.

28

Pole weapons were used by the samurai. The *naginata* was a long pole with a curved blade on the end. This was an important weapon which needed speed and skill.

The weapon was good for defence. It let you keep the enemy at a distance. It stopped them coming in close to use their sword or dagger.

On horseback, it had a better chance of hitting the enemy. It was a long pole with a sharp blade.

Scan below for *Naginata* training.

6. The Ronin

A *ronin* is a samurai without a lord or master. The master paid all the costs of the samurai. The samurai was expected to stay but if he did something wrong to the master he would lose his support. The *ronin* then is homeless and has to wander from town to town. A ronin may have to become a thief to survive.

A samurai from somewhere else was ok to use. As the land became peaceful there was no need for extra samurai. The *ronin* was supposed to kill himself if his master died. Some of the *ronin* took to the road instead of being forced to kill themselves.

The story of the 47 Ronin. This is a famous tale of the *ronin* who were great warriors during the time of the shoguns.

The *ronin* planned a revenge attack for their master, Asano, who was treated badly. When Asano was made to look a fool, it was too much for him. He attacked the official named Kira with his sword. Asano was told to kill himself. He did this and his samurai were told to do the same.

Of the 400 samurai, a small group decided to get revenge. The official had a strongly protected fort, but they got in and tied up the guards. The samurai guarding the fort were not ready and were defeated. Kira was killed and his head was put on Asano's grave.

34

7. Women Samurai

Women in Japan have always learnt martial arts. They learnt to use some weapons around the home. The *naginata* was a favourite weapon. They also used the sword.

Samurai training of women was different to the males. Women did not stay warriors for the whole of their life.

If the castle was under attack it was the job of all women to help in the battle. It was total war and if they lost they would face death or slavery.

Martial arts were learnt by the samurai class of warriors. Some of these women samurai went on to lead battles and kill their enemies.

Images show them riding back from battle with the head of an enemy against their horse. A famous woman samurai was *Tomoe Gozen* who was able to fight with a sword, ride horses, and was an archer.

Another great woman samurai was *Yamakawa Futaba* who helped her husband. Yamakawa's husband was the shogun of the northern part of Japan.

Yamakawa defended the castle against the emperor's forces. After a siege they gave up.

The attackers were put in prison, and Yamakawa became important in Japanese life. She wanted to make sure that girls had an education and a better life.

40

8. An Aussie Samurai!

Japan is a rich and powerful nation. It has very hard-working people and a strong culture. Today the samurai do not exist, but the culture still sees them as rock stars.

The samurai way of loyalty and working for the master has not left the people. People join big firms and work very hard.

More than 15 years ago, a backpacker was partying and travelling in Asia for a vacation. His name was Tom and he got a rail pass around Japan. He spoke some Japanese which he had learnt at school. He loved the trip and went back to university and studied Japanese.

After becoming fluent in Japanese, Tom went job-hunting in Japan. He had a very lowly job filling cars with gasoline in a Japanese city. He was happy to get a start and then helped decorate the gas station. He helped the owner sort out ways to sell more goods. Sales went well and the oil company asked him to help other gas stations.

The oil firm then asked him if he could come back and work in Tokyo. He studied oil trading and started buying oil for the firm. He became the best at making them money. The oil firm sent him to Singapore to be in charge of their oil trading. Now when he goes back to work in Tokyo everyone in his office stands and bows very low as he passes. The Aussie Samurai is back in town! He was just 33 years old!

Word Bank

Japanese

backpacker

university

powerful

Singapore

armor

accuracy

naginata

distance

beautiful

everywhere

important

gatherers

different

peasants

merchants

protected

struggle

treatment

special

hundreds

victory

maintaining

problems

guard

soldiers

foreigners

bushido

loyalty

ancient